T0413424

On the Job

FILMMAKERS

Adding and Subtracting Mixed Numbers

Monika Davies

Consultants

Lisa Ellick, M.A.
Math Specialist
Norfolk Public Schools

Pamela Estrada, M.S.Ed.
Teacher
Westminster School District

Publishing Credits

Rachelle Cracchiolo, M.S.Ed., *Publisher*
Conni Medina, M.A.Ed., *Managing Editor*
Dona Herweck Rice, *Series Developer*
Emily R. Smith, M.A.Ed., *Series Developer*
Diana Kenney, M.A.Ed., NBCT, *Content Director*
Stacy Monsman, M.A., *Editor*
Kristy Stark, M.A.Ed., *Editor*
Kevin Panter, *Graphic Designer*

Teacher Created Materials

5301 Oceanus Drive
Huntington Beach, CA 92649-1030
http://www.tcmpub.com

ISBN 978-1-4258-5814-8
© 2018 Teacher Created Materials, Inc.
Made in China
Nordica.112017.CA21701237

Table of Contents

The Storytellers

Our world is filled with stories. Some of the greatest stories are the ones that are captured on film! But, how well do we know the people who bring these stories to life?

Every movie has a credits list that runs a mile long. But arguably, the leader behind the scenes is the filmmaker.

The average filmmaker is more than just a **director**. He or she is often the film's **producer** and **editor**. Sometimes, that person is the film's writer, too. Filmmakers are some of the best multitaskers in the movie business!

Take a look at some of today's leading filmmakers. Each person took a unique journey to arrive at his or her current career. These filmmakers work hard to include a variety of characters in their films. They are focused on making smart and innovative movies. They are artists. Some people may even call them visionaries. But most importantly, they are storytellers—Hollywood's finest.

Clapperboards help filmmakers know details about each section of recorded film.

Ava DuVernay

Filmmakers are leaders. They coach actors and supervise a crew. Everyone on set looks to them for guidance. So, a very dedicated person must sit in the director's chair.

For Ava DuVernay, being a leader comes naturally. She has said, "From a very early age, I felt comfortable leading. I did not have any problem with speaking up."

Even though DuVernay felt she had the ability and freedom to do what she wanted, her career path did not lead directly to making films. She first worked as a **publicist**. In that role, she developed her marketing expertise for big Hollywood movies. "I didn't start out thinking I could ever make films," she said. "I started out being a film lover, loving films, and wanting to have a job that puts me close to them."

DuVernay saw a lack of African-American independent films. She wanted this to change. So, she began making changes in her life. She was still working as a publicist when she began making films.

DuVernay changes the camera angle and speed to give the audience a new perspective.

DuVernay attends the TIME 100 Gala, where she is honored as one of the most influential people of the year.

LET'S EXPLORE MATH

Script pages are usually divided into eighths because the paper is 8 inches long. One page is about 1 minute of screen time.

Suppose DuVernay needs to combine some scenes. She wants each new scene to be at least 4 minutes, or 4 pages, long. Choose all of the following expressions showing page combinations with a sum of 4 or greater.

A. $1\frac{2}{8} + 2\frac{4}{8}$ **B.** $3\frac{3}{8} + \frac{7}{8}$ **C.** $2\frac{1}{8} + 2\frac{1}{8}$ **D.** $1\frac{6}{8} + 2\frac{2}{8}$

DuVernay shares her vision for the scene with lead actor David Oyelowo.

DuVernay said, "[I] gave myself permission to go slowly. I didn't beat myself up for the fact that I had a day job. I considered how I could strengthen myself through my day job so that one was feeding the other."

In 2006, she released her first **short**, *Saturday Night Life*. In 2010, she directed her first full-length film, *I Will Follow*. Critics loved the movie. She started to get noticed for her work.

In 2014, DuVernay's film, *Selma*, released. *Selma* tells the story of Martin Luther King Jr.'s march from Selma to Montgomery, Alabama. This march was part of the movement to secure equal voting rights for all people of color.

The film's budget was $20 million. It was a big project. It came with fresh challenges. In the movie, the march is a pivotal moment. For this scene, DuVernay had to coordinate hundreds of **extras** and use a **green screen** effectively. This was new to her. But she said, "I just approached it the same way I approach any scene—what is the story here?" Her focus on the story helped bring the scene to life.

"A TRIUMPH... OYELOWO'S PERFORMANCE AS MARTIN LUTHER KING IS STUNNING"

BAZ BAMIGBOYE, DAILY MAIL

DAVID OYELOWO

SELMA

TOM WILKINSON   CARMEN EJOGO   WITH TIM ROTH   AND OPRAH WINFREY

ONE DREAM CAN CHANGE THE WORLD

IN CINEMAS 6TH FEBRUARY

Facebook.com/SelmaFilmUK   PLAN B   INGENIOUS

QUEEN SUGAR
EXECUTIVE PRODUCED BY
AVA DUVERNAY AND OPRAH WINFREY

DuVernay celebrates the premiere of the film *Queen Sugar*.

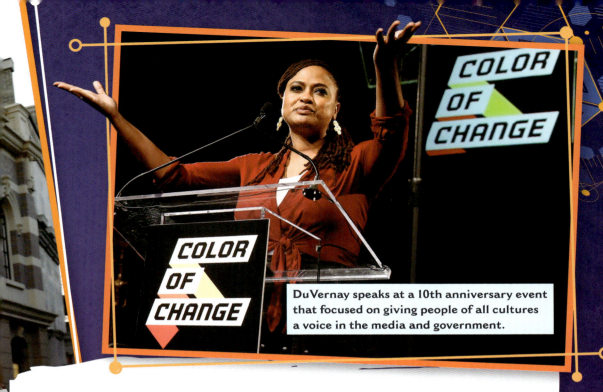

DuVernay speaks at a 10th anniversary event that focused on giving people of all cultures a voice in the media and government.

In 2015, *Selma* was nominated for Best Picture at the Academy Awards. Its success opened doors for her. But, DuVernay creates her own opportunities. She reminds us, "It's not about knocking on closed doors. It's about building our own house and having our own door."

She now has a large list of projects, including, *A Wrinkle in Time*, a big-budget **adaptation** of the classic novel. Her show, *Queen Sugar*, has been watched by many people. It airs on Oprah Winfrey's *OWN*© network.

Filmmakers often start with stories that are close to their hearts. These tales highlight events that they believe need to be given attention. For DuVernay, her films speak to what is important to her.

She says that is when she knew "that I just need to go out and tell my story, then things really changed for me. It's just knowing that there's nothing that anyone can give me that I can't do for myself in regards to my films." She went on to explain, "I want to be defined as a 'black woman filmmaker' because that's the lens through which I'm working. That is my gaze. I'm proud of it."

Justin Lin

Justin Lin's name tops the credits of some of the biggest box office flicks. He has revved up engines in the *Fast & Furious* series. In 2016, he directed the movie *Star Trek Beyond*. Lin likes to **reboot** old, favorite films and he has turned it into an art form.

Lin's family moved from Taiwan when he was young. His father was a pilot. But when they arrived in the United States, his family started a fish-and-chips shop to make money. Lin's parents worked 12-hour days. Now, Lin uses that same work ethic and focus to make films.

"Film is [like] a basketball game," he said. "When that buzzer sounds, win or lose, the only thing you can control is how much effort you put into it."

He burst onto the filmmaking scene with his 2002 **indie** debut, *Better Luck Tomorrow*. It featured an all Asian-American cast. The movie caused a stir. Roger Ebert, a top film critic, named Lin "a rising star."

Lin attends the London premiere of *Star Trek Beyond*.

While Lin's main focus is now filmmaking, he was a pretty good basketball player as a kid. Imagine that Lin plays $8\frac{1}{6}$ minutes in the first quarter and $4\frac{2}{3}$ minutes in the second quarter of a basketball game.

1. Does Lin play more or less than $12\frac{1}{2}$ minutes altogether? How do you know?

2. Choose all of the following numbers that could be used as a common denominator to find Lin's total number of minutes.

   A. 6   **B.** 12   **C.** 9   **D.** 18

3. Find the total number of minutes Lin plays in both quarters. Explain how you know your answer is reasonable.

Lin watches the action unfold from behind the camera.

"Action to me is no fun if it's not built around character," Lin explains. His success is tied directly to his focus on character.

At times, Lin works with large **ensembles**. In *Star Trek Beyond*, he juggled a big cast of characters. Yet, he made sure that each character had "valid feelings and emotional connections to the audience." He wanted to make sure that viewers felt like they had "a great relationship with all these characters."

Lin helps an actor connect with her character's emotions.

Lin poses with the cast of *Star Trek Beyond*.

Despite Lin's list of films that have done well, some of them have not been big hits. But, he embraces these misses. "We make movies and we all try our best, and sometimes we connect with the audience, sometimes we don't." He summarizes, "We will all fall, and we will all get up, and we will learn."

Lin continues to accept new projects. He likes to work, even though his job is demanding.

"Do what you love," Lin advises young filmmakers. "At the end of the day, if the film is made for the right reasons, then there's no failure."

LET'S EXPLORE MATH

Imagine that you are headed to see the latest movie from your favorite filmmaker. You earn points as a frequent moviegoer and have some points to use for your ticket and snack. Right now, you have $4\frac{1}{2}$ points. A ticket and snack deduct $1\frac{3}{4}$ points. How many points do you have left? Draw and use the model to prove your solution.

Coogler attends the premiere of *Fruitvale Station* at a film festival in Los Angeles.

Ryan Coogler

Ryan Coogler directs personal, truthful stories. Yet, he did not always want a career as a filmmaker. His college years began with him playing football. He had a football scholarship. And, he planned to become a doctor.

But during a creative writing class, his teacher had him rethinking his career path. Coogler handed in a paper about his father. After reading it, his professor told him, "I think you should become a screenwriter. You can reach more people."

At first, Coogler brushed off the idea. But, he kept thinking about stories. He began taking film classes. Soon, he veered away from football. He headed to Los Angeles for film school.

In 2013, Coogler rose to fame with his first major movie, *Fruitvale Station*. This film told the true story of the shooting of an unarmed man, Oscar Grant. The **humanity** of Coogler's film spoke to viewers.

"At the end of the day, a filmmaker's most important tool is humanity," Coogler said. "You want to be able to capture humanity in your stories, you want to be able to bring out humanity in your characters."

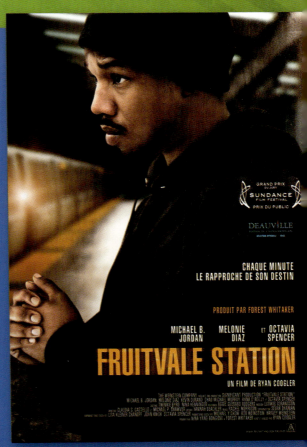

LET'S EXPLORE MATH

Suppose you start reading a book to learn more about the craft of moviemaking. On Monday, you read $2\frac{1}{4}$ chapters. On Tuesday, you read $3\frac{1}{10}$ chapters.

1. Have you read more or less than 6 chapters? How do you know?

2. Choose all of the following expressions that can be used to find the total number of chapters you have read.

   A. $2\frac{10}{40} + 3\frac{4}{40}$ **B.** $2\frac{1}{14} + 3\frac{1}{14}$ **C.** $2\frac{5}{20} + 3\frac{2}{20}$ **D.** $\frac{45}{20} + \frac{62}{20}$

3. Choose a correct expression from question 2. Use it to find how many chapters you have read. Why did you choose that expression to find the solution?

In 2015, Coogler directed *Creed*. The film was an addition to the *Rocky* series. But, this was no standard sequel. Instead, Coogler took the franchise in a new direction. He drew from his relationship with his own father to add depth to the film's story.

"[I]t's important to me to always work on projects that have things that I'm passionate about in them," he said. "This work is so all-consuming that to do this job right, you have to throw yourself at it 24 hours a day for years at a time."

Coogler demonstrates a boxing stance for the lead actor, Sylvester Stallone.

LET'S EXPLORE MATH

Suppose Coogler buys 11 pizzas for his crew. He gets a little hungry on the way, so the crew now has $10\frac{1}{3}$ pizzas to eat.

1. How much of a pizza did Coogler eat? How do you know?

2. In only a few minutes, the crew devours $8\frac{3}{4}$ of the remaining pizza. How much pizza is left over? Show your solution strategy.

Coogler poses at the premiere of *Creed*.

Coogler became a filmmaker to "tell movies that came from the perspective of characters...that I wanted to watch." His goal is to create movies that reflect "the world we live in."

Coogler's career is growing, but he tries to stay grounded. "As an artist, your greatest responsibility is to yourself," he said. "If the work you're doing doesn't mean something to you, it's not going to be good work."

Brandy Menefee: An Interview

Brandy Menefee has been working in Hollywood for over 15 years. Here, she shares her career insights and advice for getting started in filmmaking!

Author: You are a director, a producer, a writer, and an editor! What are the main differences between these roles?

Menefee: Producing is like setting the table for a big meal. Directing is like being the conductor. Editing is taking a big pile of stuff and figuring out what to do with it. Writing is where it all starts. It's your vision. This is studied by a producer to determine budget, crew, cast, and schedule.

Author: Which one is your favorite role?

Menefee: One of the things I love most about my work is the variety of opportunities. It's very hard to choose just one role that's my favorite. Directing comes naturally to me. Producing pushes me to face challenges and find solutions. I love the simplicity of writing. It's just me and my words.

Editing feels like it combines all of those roles in one. You're the final writer of the story. You're orchestrating (directing) all the shots...and doing whatever it takes (producing) to achieve a shared goal.

EYEWITNESS WAR

PROD. EYEWITNESS WAR

ROLL A/8B

SCENE WESTON OLSON INT TV

TAKE I

DIRECTOR B. MENEFEE

CAMERA C. LEALOS

DATE 5.03.13

FILTER

DAY NIGHT INT EXT MOS SYNC

Brandy Menefee

Menefee films people for a documentary film about breeding rats.

Author: You work as a storyteller in a documentary, too. What does that mean?

Menefee: I profile people, and I document their milestones. This involves interviewing people and filming parts of their lives. Then, I edit those pieces together. Finally, I present it in a way that inspires and moves people.

Sometimes people associate *documentary* with only serious subjects. But, you can create meaningful content that's also light, fun, and makes someone crack a smile.

Imagine that Brandy is working on her latest documentary. Yesterday, she spent $8\frac{2}{5}$ hours sending emails, making phone calls, and interviewing people. Today, she's been in her dark room editing for $6\frac{1}{2}$ hours. Brandy thinks she worked $14\frac{9}{10}$ hours over the last two days. Her assistant's report says $\frac{149}{10}$ hours. Explain how Brandy and her assistant are both correct. How would you choose to show the number of hours Brandy works? Why?

Author: Tell me about a day in the life of a documentary storyteller.

Menefee: Some days are all emails and phone calls.

Some days, I'm buried in a dark room editing for hours. I'm making creative decisions in front of a computer screen. And I'm hoping someone brings me a snack.

Some days, I'm trying to create a safe space for people I'm interviewing.

A perk of my job is getting to meet fascinating people. I get to explore their world and live in it. And I get to learn from them.

Author: What are some of your favorite film projects?

Menefee: I directed Channing Tatum for digital promos. I've directed some of America's top chefs and traveled all over America. And, I've lived on a tour bus for 30 days to **chronicle** the backstage **shenanigans** of an A-list musical artist.

I'm most proud of the content I created for the nonprofit Aware Awake Alive. Two parents came to me, deeply mourning the death of their son. They never wanted any family to go through their same nightmare. So, they formed a nonprofit organization and needed videos to tell their painful story. I **conceptualized**, produced, directed, and edited their story. These videos have been instrumental in the nonprofit's mission to save lives.

Brandy Menefee on set in Africa.

Author: What advice would you give your 11-year-old self about building a career in film?

Menefee: Your **point of view (POV)** is unique. It's not the best. No one's is the best. Everyone has a unique voice. Find yours. Have a POV. It doesn't have to be loud or over the top. But, your POV is what separates you from everyone else. Ten people can be assigned the same story. Each one will tell it differently. How will you tell it?

Ava DuVernay (left) and
David Oyelowo (right)

Fearless Filmmakers

Our favorite films connect with our emotions. They make us laugh and cry. They make us think about the world. Quite simply, our favorite films create magic onscreen. Dynamic filmmakers are the people behind that magic.

The one trait that ties these directors together is their commitment. They put passion and energy into their work. Filming days are long. Directors often work before the sun rises. They often continue after everyone has gone to sleep.

But, directors are usually more than willing to commit to this heavy workload. They are doing what they love. They have important stories they want to tell. Their films grow from their drive to be storytellers.

Ava DuVernay, Justin Lin, Ryan Coogler, and Brandy Menefee all work hard to make movie magic. They are committed to being leaders in their field.

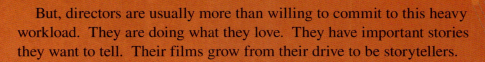

LET'S EXPLORE MATH

Over a weekend, you decide to start writing your first movie script. You write $3\frac{1}{8}$ pages on Saturday. On Sunday, you write $4\frac{2}{3}$ pages.

1. How many pages have you written?

2. How many more pages did you write on Sunday than on Saturday?

Actor Vin Diesel (left) and Justin Lin (right) discuss a scene while filming *Fast and Furious*.

Problem Solving

Filmmakers do not make movie magic alone. They have crews that help. Imagine you are the assistant director for an upcoming film. One of your responsibilities is to make sure everyone sticks to the shooting schedule. This timetable for filming keeps everyone on track. Prove that you understand the production plan by using the shooting schedule to answer the questions.

1. How many months will be spent in pre-production and shooting/filming?

2. How many months will be spent in development and post-production?

3. How much longer is development than the total amount of time needed for the other three stages?

4. What is the total amount of time planned for the shooting schedule? Is this amount of time greater than or less than 2 years? How do you know?

Shooting Schedule	
Stage of Work	**Time Needed**
development	$14\frac{7}{8}$ months
pre-production	$3\frac{2}{6}$ months
shooting/filming	$2\frac{1}{2}$ months
post-production	$6\frac{1}{4}$ months

Glossary

adaptation—a movie, book, or play that is changed to be presented in another form

chronicle—to describe events in order

conceptualized—formed an idea

director—a person who manages an organized group of people in a movie or play

editor—a person whose job it is to correct or revise something, including in film and writing

ensembles—groups of people, such as singers, actors, and dancers, who work together in a performance

extras—people hired as background actors to make scenes realistic

green screen—a large screen used as a backdrop, which is then replaced by digital images

humanity—the condition of being human

indie—a movie produced by an independent movie studio, usually with a small budget

point of view (POV)—a way of thinking about something; perspective

producer—a person who raises or pays the money to make a movie

publicist—a person whose job is to provide information about an important or famous person to the media

reboot—to create an updated version of an established series

shenanigans—silly or mischievous behavior or activities

short—a film that runs less than an hour

Index

References

Davies, Monika. 2016. "Personal Interview with Brandy Menefee."

Dockterman, Eliana. 2015. "Creed Director Ryan Coogler on His Chemistry With Michael B. Jordan." Time. http://time.com/.

Kantor, Jessica. 2016. "Ava DuVernay Shares Her Advice for Women to Break Glass Ceilings: 'Focus on Your Work.'" Glamour. http://www.glamour.com/.

Kestel, Craig. 2012. "Ryan Coogler." Filmmaker Magazine. http://filmmakermagazine.com/.

Gross, Terry. 2015. "The Sounds, Space And Spirit Of 'Selma': A Director's Take." NPR. http://www.npr.org/.

Hill, Logan. 2016. "Meet Justin Lin, the Most Important Blockbuster Director You've Never Heard Of." Wired. https://www.wired.com/.

Horn, John. 2015. "Creed Director Ryan Coogler on Reimagining Rocky and Convincing Stallone." Vulture. http://www.vulture.com/.

Mistry, Anupa. 2014. "An Interview with Ava DuVernay, Groundbreaking Director of Selma." Jezebel. http://jezebel.com/.

Ryan, Mike. 2013. "Justin Lin: James Franco's Comments About 'Annapolis' Were 'Hurtful.'" The Huffington Post. http://www.huffingtonpost.com/.

Sankin, Aaron. 2012. "'Fruitvale,' Oscar Grant Movie, To Premiere At Sundance." The Huffington Post. http://www.huffingtonpost.com/.

Smiley, Tavis. 2012. "Filmmaker Ava DuVernay." PBS. http://www.pbs.org/.

Staff. 2007. "'Finishing the Game' Director Justin Lin." IndieWire. http://www.indiewire.com/.

Staff. 2016. "Justin Lin/Star Trek Beyond Interview." YOMYOMF. https://www.yomyomf.com/.

Weintraub, Steve. 2016. "'Star Trek Beyond': Director Justin Lin on How His Approach Differs from J.J. Abrams." Collider. http://collider.com/.

Williams, Brennan. "Ava DuVernay On Why She's Not Ashamed Of Labeling Herself A 'Black Woman Filmmaker.'" The Huffington Post. http://www.huffingtonpost.com/.

Answer Key

Let's Explore Math

page 7:

B, C, D

page 13:

1. Justin plays more than $12\frac{1}{2}$ minutes because $8 + 4$ is 12, and $\frac{2}{3}$ is greater than half before adding $\frac{1}{6}$.

2. A, B, D

3. $12\frac{5}{6}$ or equivalent

page 15:

$2\frac{3}{4}$; models will vary, example:

page 17:

1. Less than 6 chapters; $2 + 3$ is 5, but $\frac{1}{4}$ and $\frac{1}{10}$ are both less than half. So, the fractions will not have the sum of 1 that would be needed for a total of 6 chapters.

2. A, C, D

3. A has a sum of $5\frac{14}{40}$; C has a sum of $5\frac{7}{20}$; D has a sum of $\frac{107}{20}$. Responses will vary but may include: I chose C because it was the most efficient for me to calculate.

page 18:

1. $\frac{2}{3}$; Responses will vary but may include: There are $10\frac{1}{3}$ pizzas left and $\frac{2}{3}$ more will be a total of 11 pizzas.

2. $1\frac{7}{12}$; Strategies will vary but may include finding common denominators, writing mixed numbers as improper fractions, or drawing a model.

page 23:

Responses will vary but may include: Brandy is correct because she used a common denominator of 10 and calculated with mixed numbers. Her assistant is also correct because $14\frac{9}{10}$ is equal to $\frac{149}{10}$. The assistant calculated with improper fractions. I would choose Brandy's way because it's easier to see that she worked more than 14 hours.

page 27:

1. $7\frac{19}{24}$ or equivalent

2. $1\frac{13}{24}$ or equivalent

Problem Solving

1. $5\frac{5}{6}$ or equivalent

2. $21\frac{1}{8}$ or equivalent

3. $2\frac{19}{24}$ or equivalent

4. $26\frac{23}{24}$ or equivalent; This is greater than two years or 24 months.